CHRISTIAN DIOR

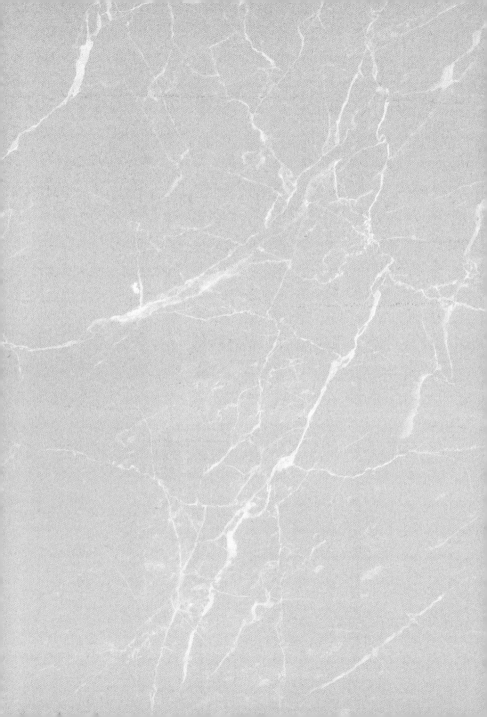

CHRISTIAN DIOR

THE STYLE PRINCIPLES

HANNAH ROGERS

Unofficial and unauthorized

Simon Element

New York   London   Toronto   Sydney   New Delhi

Intro

duction

Dior.

What comes to mind when you read that name? Chances are you have heard of it. Perhaps you have stood outside a shop window, admiring the sartorial treasures within. You might have been to an exhibition about it or come to know it a little through a documentary or film (on the subject of which, I urge you to watch *Dior and I*. It will give you a real taste of life working in haute couture).

Maybe you are someone who has long followed and admired the brand. In which case, it could summon a sentiment: of desire, wonder, and delight. A silhouette may come to mind—one, in particular, of a waspish waist. Or perhaps the name makes you think of the man himself: Christian Dior, the visionary fashion architect and master couturier, who reigned in fashion for just a decade and died in 1957, yet is still influencing how we get dressed today.

Dior certainly means something to me. It is perhaps my favorite luxury brand. I am a fully grown woman but go gooey-eyed at its creations. I have lusted after its accessories since I first started subscribing to glossy magazines and often have the Dior girl in mind when I get dressed. And, really, that's what this book is about.

Its aim is to help you get to know the man, the brand—and the look. It's got a bit of history woven in (which I hope you'll find as interesting as I did) but is certainly not an encyclopedic approach to Dior's life. No, what it does is break down the legendary fashion house's codes to help you find them in your own wardrobe, so that you, too, can create Dior-inspired ensembles at home.

Suffice it to say, I had plenty of material to work with. Despite his relatively short career—Dior was founded in 1946 and the man himself died of a heart attack aged fifty-two in 1957—Christian Dior is remembered as a revolutionary. He had strong opinions on what he considered good taste and he wasn't worried about sharing them, publishing his A-Z thoughts in his 1954 guide, *The Little Dictionary of Fashion*.

His couture broke new ground, not just for its technical techniques but also for its aesthetic. He ushered romance back into fashion at a time, just after World War II, when soberness reigned. He reinstated luxury—real, in-your-face opulence—when rationing and austerity were words of the day. As for the boxy, gamine tailoring women had taken to in the thirties and forties thanks to one Coco Chanel . . . well, you need only see the cinched hourglass figures of his first collection—duly dubbed the "New Look" by an excited *Harper's Bazaar*'s Carmel Snow—to see what he thought of that.

Dior was a fantasist—in the times he could afford to be and the times, perhaps, he had to be. He grew up relatively well-off in the lavish belle époque but later faced periods of failure, hardship, and poverty. It took him until he

Dior seamstresses reading the shocking news
of Christian Dior's death at the age of fifty-two.

was in his thirties to embark on the career that would make him the hallowed name in fashion he is today. There were always signs he would get there, though: he spent his life admiring the finer things, from architecture and gardens to music and art.

He certainly would not have predicted that he might go on to dress royalty, nor that his take on hemlines would come to be known around the world. It was a fact he sometimes separated himself from—putting Christian Dior the man in one box and Christian Dior the couturier in another. Despite the fact that a fortune teller had told him, at age thirteen, that he'd make his fortune from women, it still took him by surprise when he did.

There's no shortage of magic in the story of Christian Dior. That's why so many fall under its spell. The clothes are bewitching, but—beneath the layers of tulle—so is their creator's surprisingly practical take on getting dressed. His style principles are a story of quality over quantity, the importance of individuality, and dressing to feel your absolute best. It's a set of ideas we can all apply to our own wardrobes. This book will show you how.

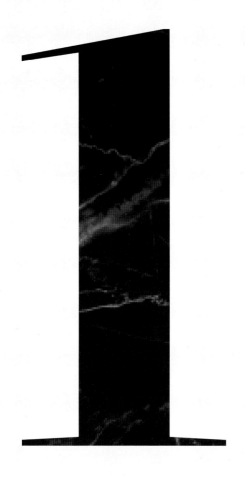

1

Learn your
LINES

"A dress is a piece of ephemeral architecture, designed to enhance the proportions of the female body."

Christian Dior

Designer. Dream-maker. Fantasy-frock fabricator and real-life-princess outfitter. Christian Dior is a name in fashion that evokes full-on, gooey reverie. It is a brand that conjures up pictures of sartorial magic: the stuff of frothy tulle, painstakingly handsewn embellishment, and stiff, shiny taffeta. It has, since its inception in 1946, stood for the utmost glamour, for femininity at its most delicate, and for elegance that is unparalleled.

Dior, to my mind, is fashion at its most romantic. It is the brand that pirouetted through my subconscious when I was choosing my wedding dress (no surprise I ended up falling for one with a nipped-in, belted waist and enormous petticoat-propped skirt). Its clothes to this day remain fit for a fairy tale, from toile de Jouy printed silk separates to floor-sweeping gowns. Add to that the fact that most people could only dream of owning one of its coveted items, and the sentiment of myth and fantasy is sealed. Dior is the stuff of legend.

Unlike the best-known fables, though, its story does not pivot around the comings and goings of a princess, wicked stepmother, or handsome prince. It does not actually even begin with a designer. That's because Christian Dior, the man credited with changing how women in the postwar era got dressed, did not expect to end up working in the world of haute couture. Actually, he wanted to be an architect.

I'm not making it up. The fact is that Dior never set out, in his formative years, to be a dressmaker. He was thirty years old before he started to sketch his own clothing; a bit older than that when he landed his first job in haute couture. He did not spend his happy and comfortable childhood dreaming of dressing women, nor were his adolescent thoughts consumed by hemlines, silhouettes, and seams.

No, what got Dior going—not just as a child, but throughout his life—was architecture. It was a self-professed weakness (one he later used the profits from his fashion house to satisfy by buying and renovating various homes) and a passion he had always wanted to pursue. Had his parents not stood in his way—instead suggesting that he study political science (a degree he flopped out of anyway to get into modern art)—we might never have heard of Christian Dior, haute couturier. He'd have more likely put his name to building design.

Fashionistas certainly have much to thank his parents for. But, actually, so does Dior. For while he may not have ended up an architect of bricks and mortar, he certainly did of garments and—if you'll allow me a bit of whimsy—of dreams. He said himself that couture became an outlet for his primary passion. Instead of bridges and buildings, he built internal structures for skirts. The tailoring used to make his jackets and frocks was so technical, it was said the items could stand up on their own. And just like any building, every design started with a blueprint: that of the idealized female form—a perfect hourglass ratio of hips, waist, and bust. Dior collections celebrated it to extremes.

Every single one of Dior's collections had an extremely specific and dramatic silhouette—what he referred to as his "lines." How they were achieved goes back to the architecture of his couture. Fierce underpinnings and singular craftsmanship gave Dior designs a distinct profile. It's what earned him his reputation and swift success, and brought into the world that most revolutionary of debut collections: what is still known to this day as the New Look.

More on that later. The point of this chapter—Dior's very first style principle—is to learn about those lines. They can tell us much about how the curves of the body featured in the design process and their forefront position in the couturier's mind. With that aim, what follows are a few outlines of Dior's twenty-two collections. You won't struggle to work out how his original passion and fashion became intertwined.

"Corolle" and *'8 Lines'*
(Spring/Summer 1947)

The original hourglass, Dior's first collection was split into two sections, both boasting molded busts, minuscule wasp waists, and full skirts so long and swishy that they knocked over editors' ashtrays as the models turned. Everything about it was novel (hence it coming to be known as the New Look): the sheer yardage of fabric each look used was considered scandalously lavish and its shapes were an ultra-feminine departure from the boxy, boyish shapes Coco Chanel had kept in vogue.

"Zig-zag" & "Envol"
(Spring/Summer 1948)

A collection that aimed to give the look of a drawing. Looks focused less on the chest, more on the waist, and skirt details fell to the back, while fabric, supported by inner trappings, appeared to literally take flight. In layman's terms: it had volume.

"Trompe l'œil"
(Spring/Summer 1949)

"Trompe l'oeil" in the most literal sense means "to deceive the eye" and is common parlance among personal stylists who make a living out of flattering the body. In this collection, pieces came with bust-widening tops, while clever floating panels on skirts gave the illusion of fullness to what was actually a smooth, clean silhouette.

Other lines

VERTICAL LINE

Less volume, more bodycon: narrowly molded busts, nipped waists, and tighter skirts for daytime.

OBLIQUE LINE

"Oblique" means "slanting," which is exactly what looks in this collection appeared to be, thanks to diagonal cuts and wonky details such as large vertical pockets, asymmetric necklines, and almost S-shaped buttoning.

NATURAL LINE

A sharp move away from the New Look, this collection was not set on exaggerating the female form, but following it: far easier to wear but still unarguably elegant.

LONG LINE

The favorite of all Dior's collections and a follow-on from the natural line, but with longer skirts that covered the calf and neat, cropped peplum jackets that emphasized them.

TULIP LINE

A testament to his love of flowers, the tulip line mimicked the shape of its namesake, with narrow hips and rounded, prominent, petallike busts.

LIVING LINE

Inspired by the Paris skyline, this collection featured frocks that simulated the shape of the Eiffel Tower and the city's cupolas (domes).

H, A, AND Y LINES

Collections that followed the shape of said alphabet letters. The H was hip-based; the A line called for a narrow top that flared out down the body. The Y brought the waist higher on the body and accented the bust.

SPINDLE LINE

The designer's final collection before his death a few months later was designed to fit within the shape of two brackets—i.e., ( )—and featured unwaisted, loose-fitting looks among bell-skirted gowns and flapper-style dresses.

Oblique line

Natural line

Tulip line

A line

Don't feel you have to commit all this to memory. It's unlikely you'll ever be quizzed on every silhouette Dior championed. But understanding how important his lines were to him—how distinct they were each season; how thought through—is something you can take into your own wardrobe.

It comes down to the figures they cut. Body shape was everything to Dior. Whether he was exaggerating parts of it or creating clothes that followed its natural lines, the fit and how he could best flatter clients with his fashions consumed him.

So the first Dior style principle, I think, is understanding one's own figure—and how clever styling tricks can make the most of it.

The simplest way to get started is to **get your hands on a full-length mirror**. Stand in front of it and consider what you see. Is your body curved? Straight? Rounded here and inverted there? Getting comforta-

ble with your body in all its glory is the first step to better grasping and celebrating its shape. You can also use a tape measure (or ribbon or string if you prefer to avoid numeric measurements) to work out any ratios if you want to get technical.

There are professionals that can help in this department, too, if it is something you would really like to dig into. **Personal stylists** offering body mapping will stand you against a piece of large brown paper and mark your silhouette, identifying all the key lengths, measurements, ratios, and proportions that signpost your body shape. One such expert is the London-based Anna Berkeley, who gives her clients nine body types to consider.

She says that most people are a blend of body shapes but have a dominant one to work off. Understanding proportions, body sections, and frame alongside a sense of overall shape is the key.

Body shape

hourglass

Dior's ideal—a defined waist with full bust, bottom, and hips, where the bust and hip are roughly equal.

bottom hourglass

A curvy shape where the bottom and hips are fuller than the bust.

top hourglass

A curvy shape where the bust is fuller than the hip and thigh.

rounded

A rounded shoulder line, fullness around the middle, and a flat bottom.

column

Straight up-and-down, with shoulders roughly equal to hips.

rectangle

Straight up-and-down but broader.

triangle

A fuller bottom half (hips and thighs), a defined waist, and smaller bust.

inverted triangle

The opposite—a straight shape, square shoulders, little to no waist, and a smaller lower half.

spoon

A straighter upper body and gently curving hip, bottom, and thigh.

Keep in mind that every body is, wonderfully, different. Don't get hung up on the shape and size—it's only part of the picture. A body really is just that.

All that said, you might just prefer not to get into labels. Fair enough. In which case, here are five quick styling tips that work universally.

1
A flash of ankle
is always a good idea — but where the hem of your skirt,
dress, or trousers falls is vital. It should be at the smallest
point of your leg: usually to show off the entire ankle bone
and a slice of leg.

2
V-necks
are universally flattering but work super well
on those with round faces and larger busts.

3
Pattern, color, and embellishment
can make areas look larger, so use them for elements
you'd like to draw attention to (and vice versa, avoid them
where you'd rather not). Or use them as a balancer —
for instance, if you are larger on top, only wear
a pattern on the lower half.

4
Vertical stripes
will elongate.

5
Full skirts
will make your waist and shoulders look smaller,
as well as enhance the bust.

Don't shy away from getting
to know your figure—having
the tools to make the most
of yourself is empowering.
That might feel like a dated
idea, but the body positivity
movement is all about
celebrating what you have, and
I don't think understanding
your shape negates that.

There's nothing wrong, to
my mind, with dressing to
feel good about yourself and
having a few tricks up your
sleeve to help you do so. Dior
himself said that happiness
was the secret to all beauty.
What could make you happier
than looking and feeling your
very best?

Pick your
PRINT

"Individuality will always be one of the conditions of real elegance."

Christian Dior

S oftness, femininity, glamour, and grace. It's not hard to imagine what words were pinned to Christian Dior's mood board. A garment's practicality was not his main concern when designing; his romantic and refined couture had one goal: to make women look and feel (in Dior's eyes) beautiful. But a frock alone was not enough to achieve that. The designer had opinions and suggestions on all other matters aesthetic, too.

This ranged from hairstyles (nothing too complicated that you couldn't do yourself; absolutely no dye—not even when you go gray) and handbags (keep them simple in the daytime; never overfill them) to hemlines (where they fall should vary on the individual). Now, that's just the *H*s. The man wrote an entire dictionary of fashion advice in 1954, an A–Z guide for women to refer to if ever in doubt of what determined good taste. There was no limit to the areas where Dior could offer counsel to ensure a woman could put her—to his mind—best (heeled) foot forward. Don't worry, we'll get to the shoes in a later chapter.

So it will come as no surprise that these robust opinions applied to patterns and prints. Dior often used motifs in his work—some that may seem obviously fitting with the fashion house codes and others not. Take florals as an example of the former. They were one of the couturier's favored emblems that really embody the sort of old-school femininity we might associate with Dior. The garden was a huge source of inspiration for the designer; he referred to his clients as "flower women," and one collection, the 1954 haute couture line, was entirely devoted to the lily of the valley. It came in hues of lilac and was patterned in the pretty, delicate flower.

But it is not those ditsy blooms that I am particularly interested in. Nothing wrong with florals, of course—they have their merits, particularly come wedding season—but there are two other Dior patterns that I think have a bit more bite. The first is leopard and the second is houndstooth. Both have been a feature at the house since its very first collection and have rich stories to tell not just about Dior himself, but his take on style. Let's start with leopard.

Dior Spring Collection, 1958.

Marlene Dietrich

Hollywood icon Marlene Dietrich enthusiastically adopted all of Dior's creations. It was pretty much the only designer she wore, and she once famously told the director Alfred Hitchcock before filming began on *Stage Fright* in 1950: "No Dior, no Dietrich!"

Leopard print

Love it or loathe it—and leopard print certainly is one of those looks that provokes strong opinions—big-cat spots have been part of Dior's story from the beginning. The designer introduced his "jungle" print—an exclusive take on the beige and black motif designed by the eponymous Lyons-based silk-weaving manufacturer Bianchini Férier—on two looks in his first collection, most notably a belted, short-sleeve dress with a body-hugging, calf-length skirt. The model wearing it carried a matching leopard-print coat in her hand; the oblong buckle of the belt was also duly spotted.

The markings appeared time and again in his subsequent collections. Dior pioneered his jungle print: he used it to create dramatic looks not just designed for cocktail hour, but also for afternoon tea. He thought it worked particularly well for statement outerwear, too, creating one such trench coat in the 1950s that was enthusiastically adopted by the German American actress Marlene Dietrich. He was also responsible for the leopard-print one-piece worn by the French ballet dancer, singer, and actress Zizi Jeanmaire in the 1957 film *Too Many Lovers*.

Dior's zeal for leopard was twofold. First, it speaks to his place as a post-World War II designer. Haute couture experienced a creative revival in the years that followed the German surrender in 1945. Designers of the era were injecting joy and playfulness back into fashion after years of rationing and hardship. Embracing a bold print played into that—it was fun.

Second, it was the signature look of his most beloved muse. Mitzah Bricard was a woman who, in Dior's eyes, embodied elegance. If chic was a language, she was naturally and effortlessly fluent. She had a je ne sais quoi that could not be learned and he looked to her for inspiration and advice throughout his ten years at the helm of his house, which was easy enough to do. She worked there as his head of millinery.

Bricard was famous for wearing leopard print: on a silk scarf around her wrist, on her favorite veiled hats, on coats. Her way with it—and, more to the point, the way she wore it—sent Dior into raptures. It is no coincidence that he was quick to adopt it in his designs. Without her, leopard print would have never become a regular feature at the house.

Mitzah Bricard

Mitzah Bricard, born Germaine Louise Neustadt on November 12, 1900, started her career at Dior as a patternmaker in 1946 and quickly made an impression. "Bricard is one of those people, increasingly rare, who make elegance their sole reason for being," Dior wrote in his autobiography. It is understood that she lived at the Ritz, would cruise into the Avenue Montaigne atelier around noon—always in her turban, pearls, high heels, and also, reportedly, often commando—and make audacious demands and candid comments on looks in production. Dior adored her.

Leopard print has been reimagined numerous times under Dior's many creative directors. Marc Bohan created suits of leopard-printed mink fur for his 1972 haute couture collection. John Galliano, the most avant-garde designer to helm the brand (between 1996 and 2011), turned it into eight blingy urban-jungle looks for his Autumn/ Winter 2000 collections (think clingy, bias-cut slip dresses, ripped jeans, and fur-collar Afghan coats all presented on a gold mirrored catwalk).

Maria Grazia Chiuri revived leopard again after becoming creative director in 2016, renaming it the "Mizza" print (after Bricard), reinventing it in bright hues and splashing it across bags, scarves, shoes, and ready-to-wear. It was worn head to toe in a 2023 beauty campaign with the actress Anya Taylor-Joy—in the limited-edition collection she promoted, it even came printed on the make-up palettes. *Rawr.*

Houndstooth

Dior loved checks. Stylistically speaking, he thought they ticked every box. But it was houndstooth that he admired the most. He used the black-on-white, jagged-diagonal weave time and again in his collections and it remained in creative rotation with his successors. Marc Bohan used it for his sixties suiting; Raf Simons stuck it on bustiers and two-tone frocks. These days you can find it being used far beyond the brand's tailoring department—it comes on kitten heels, hoodies, and handbags, too.

As for the original couturier, he loved it for its optical effects. But he also loved the Englishness of it. You might not know that Dior—who perhaps to many might be the very embodiment of a chic *Parisien*— was in fact a great Anglophile. He adored England. From his first visit in 1926 (as a last hurrah before military service), he was seduced by the country and its people.

He returned many times, for work and pleasure, later setting up a licensing business in London. He thought English women prettier than any others and traditional British textiles equally pleasing. He was effusive about the way in which the likes of houndstooth, tweeds, and Prince of Wales checked fabrics fell and were cut, and enjoyed taking what were then considered traditionally masculine fabrics and turning them into ladylike pieces for the Dior woman.

Four looks in his first collection were made from houndstooth fabric: the Montmartre, Rien, Oxford, and Promenade. For the Spring/Summer 1951 collection, a coat was designed in a pale blue version of the print. And when his Miss Dior perfume launched in 1947, the designer embossed houndstooth onto the bottles, an idea returned to in February 2022 when the print was stamped onto a limited-edition set of lipsticks.

Pulling off prints

Now you know the prints, let's discuss how to wear them. I think the first question to ask is: How does the print make you feel? By which I mean, do you think it's something you could wear top to toe—indeed, would you even want to?

Dior felt that pulling off a print hinged on the individual wearing it. On this point, I have to agree. That's less about a print suiting you, though, and more about whether wearing something eye-catching excites you. If you are not someone who would usually opt for a full-on look, don't feel that you have to start now. Mitzah Bricard we are all not. Besides, it is very easy to adopt print in small ways that are nonetheless both stylish and effective. Read on for three simple tips.

PAIR WITH PLAIN

Let's assume you've chosen one item—a top, coat, skirt, pair of trousers, or even a dress—in your print of choice. Marvelous. Now, keep the rest of your outfit simple, in complementary block colors. This will, on the one hand, make the print stand out and, on the other, stop it from tipping into over the top (OTT) territory. Worn like this, it will feel as much of a neutral as the rest of your look.

USE TO YOUR ADVANTAGE

Prints can be worn to draw attention to and away from other parts of the body. You may not wish to do either, of course, but it is worth thinking about. (Refer back to Anna Berkeley's tips in chapter one.)

IF IN DOUBT, START SMALL

Accessories are the perfect gateway to prints: you can't go wrong with a leopard- or houndstooth-print shoe, scarf, bag, or even a hat if you want to dress up, say, a navy jumper. The best thing about leopard print and houndstooth is that they are both equally graphic and gutsy, but they are also what the most committed fashionistas would consider "neutrals." The style set is not afraid to mix clashing prints: at Fashion Week, you might find leopard spots teamed with Breton stripes or houndstooth with other checks. It might sound mad until you try it. Go on—perhaps you'll discover your inner Mitzah.

3

Embrace your
WAIST

"Without proper foundations, there can be no fashion."

Christian Dior

How does a down-on-his luck former art gallerist turned fledgling designer take up a starring role in one of the most captivating success stories—in the world of fashion or otherwise—of all time? Well, he does something different, of course. It is not something completely of his own invention—in fact, it harks back to the past (trends are circular, after all).

But in the climate in which he presents it to the world, it feels fresh. In fact, it feels groundbreaking. Which is funny when you think about it, because all that the designer really did on that fateful February afternoon in his brand-new, freshly painted dove-gray salon on the Avenue Montaigne was offer women something that they already had but had forgotten about. And until the moment they saw it, they didn't even know they wanted it back.

It's Dior's New Look silhouette I am talking about: the extreme hourglass. On February 12, 1947, Christian Dior cinched, defined, molded, and gave women back their waists.

It is impossible to talk about Dior without the waist. It was his unique selling point as a couturier and a feature of all his collections. Its significance to the designer is made quite clear in his *Little Dictionary of Fashion*. The waistline gets a generous annotation and he underlines his view that it is crucial to dressmaking. Dior felt that perfectly proportioned curves were the dream of every woman. That idea might feel dated now – not least because it comes from a man – but it gripped the world in 1947 and did not let go in the ten years Dior spent designing after that. At the epicenter of the success of that 1940s fantasy silhouette is the waist.

We need to go back a little to understand what shaped Dior's beauty ideals. There are, I think, three significant factors. The first is his mother, Madeleine Dior. Dior grew up comfortably wealthy in the heyday of belle époque – a prewar era in France characterized by excess, prosperity, and frivolity. Women's fashion was for corsets and petticoats: big busts, tiny waists, and huge skirts. Clothing was cumbersome but the movement was very much in favor of more is more: if you could move easily in your frock, it wasn't fashionably heavy enough.

Madeleine, the wife of a successful fertilizer and chemicals businessman, had a wardrobe full of such looks. It is thought that Dior's designs harked back to how she dressed, for he had admired her greatly, also inheriting his love of the garden and flowers from her. She passed away prematurely in 1930 when Dior was twenty-five years old, leaving the designer bereft. Her influence on what he considered beautiful should not be underestimated.

A classic Dior suit accentuating the waist, 1951.

Second, as we touched upon in chapter one, Dior had a predilection for fine things. He kept himself amused by sketching flowers in the garden as a child. He was initially keen on architecture: he loved structure and was fascinated by how things were built. And after his flop degree, it was contemporary art he turned his attention to, setting up a gallery with funding from his father (money that was handed over in exchange for the Dior name not going above the shop door—equal to social death in his parents' circles).

In that gallery hung the work of then little-known names like Pablo Picasso, Henri Matisse, and Salvador Dalí. It is another example of Dior being a man of taste and foresight: no surprise he ended up founding a business that relied on creativity, craftsmanship, and vision. But we need to dig into his road there a bit more. It was long, winding—and, at times, bleak. What Dior lived through not long after opening that art gallery goes some way to explaining why he approached fashion as he did: the third building block of his aesthetic tower.

In 1930 the Great Depression hit. Dior's brother was diagnosed with an incurable disease, his mother died, and, in 1931, his father lost all of the family's money. Dior's art gallery had to close; he opened another; that met the same fate. Destitute and living in attic rooms in Paris, the designer fell seriously ill and was forced to live abroad for a year in search of fresh air.

There, he leaned into working with fabrics for the first time, learning the niche art of tapestry. It gave him the nudge to apply for a job in fashion design when he did return to Paris, turning his hand to fashion illustration and eventually being offered a job as a designer in 1938 at the couture house of Robert Piguet. World War II quickly put paid to that opportunity; Dior was briefly called away to military service until 1941. It was then, finally, that he got his real break: a role in

Lucien Lelong's atelier. Working alongside Pierre Balmain (recognize that name?), Dior's life as a couturier had, at last, properly begun.

The sartorial mood at this moment in time was, like the global outlook, joyless. Clothes rationing was in place and the wealthy sought stealth-wealth outfits that didn't scream of excess. Simple, unostentatious, monochrome boxy tailoring pioneered by the likes of Coco Chanel held a firm grip. It wasn't ugly or lacking in chicness, necessarily—but fashion was certainly not having fun.

In 1946—rather out of the blue, while still happily working away at Lelong—Dior had the chance to change that. He was approached repeatedly by a wealthy textile magnate, Marcel Boussac, about reviving a couture house: that of Philippe et Gaston. After some thought, the suggestion in response from Dior was that Boussac should instead financially back a brand-new label: Maison Christian Dior. You know what happened next.

I have rattled through all that because it sets up the opening of Dior's atelier in a place in time—one in which the public was tired of the global outlook and ready for change. Haute couture experienced a great revival after World War II; the world—and, particularly, the very wealthy—was ready to embrace the vibrancy, creativity, and fancifulness that luxury designers were putting out.

Dior's New Look was very much part of that. He wanted to break away from what he saw to be the dull fashions of the day. His first collection oozed opulence and novelty not just for its silhouette, but also for its use of fabric. Each frock and skirt used an extreme amount of yardage that shocked—and excited—a society so beaten down by years of austerity. It was nothing short of scandalous, the sheer lavishness of it all. Most who saw it didn't mind at all, though—in fact, they were thrilled.

Of all the pieces Dior presented that afternoon, there is one item in particular that is hallowed at Dior: Le Bar. It brings us back to the very part of the body we want to talk about in this chapter. The Bar jacket—which, in its original form, came single-breasted in white, with soft, rounded shoulders, a nipped waist, and padded peplums that exaggerated it as part of a suit—single-handedly embodied the New Look revolution. Perhaps you have seen the famous photo of it captured in 1955 by Willy Maywald, where it is modeled with black gloves and a slanting Tonkinese hat on the banks of the Seine. The actress Elle Fanning wore a tribute to it on the red carpet in Cannes in 2019 (pictured on page 79).

The Bar was designed like a sculpture intended to enhance the female form. Still is. I tried one on when writing this book (purely for research purposes, you understand). The Bar jacket is still part of the house's core collection; there is an entire section devoted to it on the Dior website. It has been reimagined repeatedly by Monsieur Dior's successors, not just as jackets but coats and dresses. Nowadays, it comes in many forms, from classic wool and silk to more contemporary quilted and denim. The prices vary, but the bog-standard Bar typically costs in the region of £3,000.

Given that, perhaps it will please you to hear—or not, actually—that as an item of clothing, it is metamorphic. In the brief moments I wore it on my body in that heavily carpeted changing room, I could feel its craftsmanship and structure. Yet it had a softness and fluidity to it, too: it held its shape without feeling stiff. Suffice it to say, even wearing it with my jeans, I looked very expensive. Such a delight was short-lived.

Get the New Look

You don't need a Bar jacket to get a New Look silhouette. Nor does the New Look silhouette have to be the goal of getting dressed. I have mentioned that Dior's ideas on what a woman's body should look like are somewhat outdated. There is no one "right" type of figure to have now (although you don't need me to tell you that most luxury fashion designers still seem to use very slim ones as their blueprint). Further, what denotes femininity today is the subject of blistering political debate. Dior's exaggerated hourglass figure is not the be-all and end-all of womanhood or attractiveness anymore. So, how to bring this house code up to date?

The answer—I think—is by focusing on the waist, still, but not in the extreme. The perfect hourglass is not a flattering silhouette on everyone. Dior actually didn't think it was either—he was anti-trends (I know—the irony) and pro his clients wearing clothes that best suited them, fashions be damned. His looks may have cinched the waist but they were also, remember, made-to-measure. They would have been uniquely tweaked and adjusted from the original pattern to suit each of his client's specifications. Such is the nature of haute couture.

In that spirit (and on the understanding that most of us do not have access to personal seamstresses), I wanted to find out how the average consumer might go about embracing their waist, and how to make waisted looks work — if indeed they do work universally — on different figures. Here is what I learned from personal style consultant and celebrity stylist Prue White — an expert in all things fashion for every body.

USE THE RULE OF THIRDS

It is one of styling's universals, in that it works on everyone by proportionally splitting your outfit into three parts and dictating where to put visual breaks (e.g., a waistline). To do this, look in a full-length mirror and find the middle line of your body (usually just below the hips). This is often the widest section of your figure and thus most likely where you want to avoid a visible distinction (so, where your bottom meets your top, for example).

Have a look at the basic examples opposite for a better understanding.

2/3 long blazer or untucked top

1/3 top tucked in

1/3 trousers or midi skirt

CHRISTIAN DIOR

2/3 high waisted bottom

63

DON'T FORCE A WAIST

Some people are rounder through the middle and it might not be advantageous to draw a horizontal line across their central point, stylistically speaking (i.e., with a belt). In that case, opt for an empire or princess line that nips in directly under the bust.

YOU DON'T HAVE TO CINCH

Belts are an extreme option and they don't work for everyone. Slick tailoring, a peplum top (great for straight body types), or even a French tuck—where you tuck just the front part of your top into your bottoms—give the imitation of a waist. The latter is great for boxy, oversized items and creates a waistline in a contemporary way. Think about proportion, too—A-lines over the hips or broader shoulders can help create the illusion of a smaller waist on taller frames.

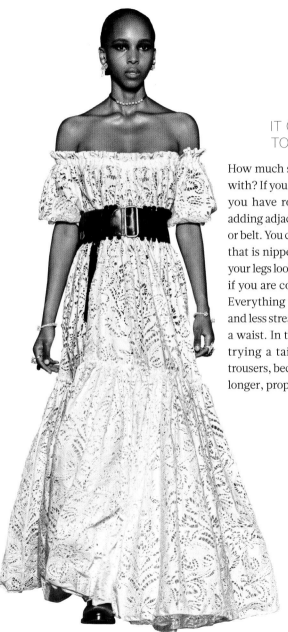

IT COMES DOWN TO REAL ESTATE

How much space do you have to work with? If you are long through the body, you have room to create a waist by adding adjacent volume with a peplum or belt. You could also try a dress or skirt that is nipped in at the waist, to make your legs look longer. That's not the case if you are compact through the body. Everything would become very bulky and less streamlined if you tried to force a waist. In this case, you are better off trying a tailored jacket or mid-rise trousers, because your legs are probably longer, proportionally speaking.

Each of the waist-centric styling methods mentioned above are mainstays on Dior catwalks. Season after season, tailoring that is at once sharp and soft—peplum flares, belts, A-line bottoms, and cropped-top-half items—have been utilized by the brand's creative directors to draw the eye to the waist.

The clever thing is that they do so without sacrificing comfort. Netflix's *Bridgerton* might have made corsets fashionable again for a hot minute, but most people don't want to be dramatically cinched-in now. Using the above tips, you've got the tools to embrace your waist—while still also being able to embrace a proper Sunday lunch.

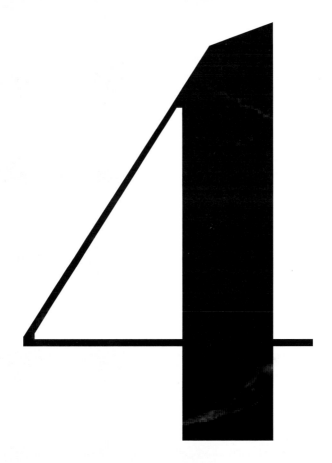

Find your
MIDI *(skirt)*

"*Real elegance
is everywhere,
especially in
the things that
don't show.*"

Christian Dior

I t is not unusual for a fashion designer to goad their audience with a provocative skirt length. But if they do manage to raise any perfectly arched eyebrows on the front row, that is usually because said skirt is short. Knicker flashing, bum-cheek hugging, thigh-grazing: these are the hemline descriptions that stereotypically cause a stir. (Google the low-rise micro kilts of Miu Miu's Spring/Summer 2022 collection if you want to see what I mean.)

Well, not in 1947 – not in the case of Dior.

In fact, if the hemline index theory is to be believed – whereby skirts get shorter in good economic times and longer in bad – economists must have whimpered at the sight of his New Look. You know by now how groundbreaking that collection was, sending not just fashionistas into a frenzy, but also the world press at large. It was the length of Dior's skirts that made headlines, and not just because they were a departure from the neat, boxy, knee-length styles in vogue at the time. They were full, vast, floor-sweeping, and so dramatically—enticingly—different that British journalists in the salon audience were seen attempting to yank the hemlines of their own skirts further down.

So what? you might think. They sound formal, prim— modest by today's standards. Why the dramatics? Certainly, there wasn't much traditionally sexy or shocking, in the modern sense, about Dior's designs. They cinched their wearer's silhouette into that alluring hourglass but they also unashamedly covered her up.

That was **exactly** the problem, though, for some women— those who had felt liberated by the shorter, more practical skirts ushered in by Chanel through the thirties. It was also a problem for the men who had become accustomed to seeing women's legs. Yes, really. Dior's skirts were particularly contentious in America for this very reason; his New Look hemlines actually sparked campaign groups against them.

The Little Below the Knee Club, founded by twenty-four-year-old Dallas housewife and former model Bobbie Wood-ward in 1947, was one such union. It spread to forty-eight states and was reportedly 1,300 strong at its first picket-line demonstration: a march through the streets, calves brazenly visible, holding placards with the rather brilliant slogan "We won't revert to grandma's skirt." The American press (not those working at glossy magazines like *Vogue* and *Harper's Bazaar*, mind—I'm talking about the testosterone-dominated newspapers) supported them wholeheartedly. You can just imagine the buzz in those cigarette-smoke-clouded newsrooms as they sniggered over their "Hem Wars" headlines.

If Dior was in any doubt over the scandal he had unintentionally caused, he got a taste of it in person when he arrived in America for the first time. He had been invited to receive an award for his first collection from the chichi department chain Neiman Marcus, a trip he assumed—forgivably, in the pre-digital age—he'd be taking in the safety of relative anonymity. No such luck. The immigration officers in New York greeted him with a hard time—over his skirts, not his passport—and ushered him onto a dock full of bulb-flashing journalists demanding that the designer defend himself for covering up their country's fine female pins.

The second stick—or perhaps ruler would be more apt—with which Dior's critics beat him when it came to his skirts was less fashion-related, more fiscal. The sheer amount of

Women protesting Dior's designs for long skirts, 1947.

fabric used to make them was considered an outrage at a time when austerity still held its cold grip on Europe. The war was over (just), but France was still recovering from German occupation in 1947. In England, clothes rationing was still in force. The head of the Board of Trade there, Sir Stafford Cripps, was firmly against the New Look purely for the fact that its garments required twice the amount of fabric as normal; he and his successor Harold Wilson urged British fashion journalists to report unfavorably on it.

Clearly none of that mattered. Dior had read the proverbial room—or, rather, salon. He predicted that the world was ready for a bit of luxury after years of frugality and, sure enough, the world embraced it. It was his intention to bring joy into women's wardrobes again and, by his second collection, that mood shift was well underway. At that time Dior said that postwar spirits were so high, it mattered not how heavy his garments were—nothing could weigh his clients down. No surprise that the so-called "tyrant of hemlines" did not rush to appease his detractors and significantly shorten his skirts. He didn't have to.

Hemlines have crept up at Dior in the decades since its founder's death. You might suggest that his passing cleared the way for Mary Quant to usher in her miniskirts six years later, in 1964 (more likely, the world was just ready for something new—no fashions last for ever). Yves Saint Laurent, who helmed the house straight after Dior's death, designed skirts that hit the knee; Marc Bohan, who took over in 1960 and stayed for twenty-nine years, took hemlines well above it.

But even under the more recent or avant-garde creative directors—John Galliano, Raf Simons, Maria Grazia Chiuri—midi skirts have been a mainstay at Dior. That doesn't mean they are staid or matronly—modern takes have come slit to the thigh, in punkish plaid, and even completely see-through. They can feel youthful, polished, playful, or professional. You just need to find the one that perfectly suits you.

Finding the skirt for you

Dior was clearly enthusiastic about longer hemlines, but he was just as dogmatic about his clients finding skirts and dresses at a length that looked best on them—and that, he said, came down to height and the style of skirt. But that was easy for him to say. He was an haute couturier: every one of his pieces was made-to-measure. When a client ordered a look from the collection, it was made to her exacting needs and personal sizing.

Most of us don't have that privilege today. We shop from racks. But Dior was correct in thinking that the right midi varies for every individual; one skirt can fall any way—and myriad ways—on different people.

I asked the fashion editor and personal stylist Annabel Hodin, who helps her clients build enhancing, real-world wardrobes, how to find, as it were, "the one." She says that everyone can pull off a midi skirt, but "it is important to balance your body shape, elongate whenever possible, and understand the shape and length of any layering jackets, cardigans or sweaters."

Hodin says that your midi should:

Balance your proportions.

●

Have a hem that sits at the slimmest part of your
leg. For most people, this is about eighteen
inches from the floor.

●

Create a silhouette that is pinched at the waist.
This can be done by tucking in a top or adding a belt.

●

Create your waist one inch up from where it normally
would be or wear one color or tone top to toe, so
as not to cut your body in half. A leg-revealing split
will also make legs look longer.

●

Your top or jacket should make up ⅓ of the whole outfit
(this is in line with the rule of thirds Prue White outlined in
the previous chapter). You should also define your shoulders, which will help create Dior's perfect 8 silhouette.

●

The rest is individual—as Dior would wish! But I do have
a few ideas if you are stuck for a style to choose. There are
five types of midi, to my mind, that fit the Dior look.
I hope outlining them might inspire you.

Tutu

Delicate, frothy, and fun, it is Maria Grazia Chiuri who has made tulle midis a house code at Dior. She has styled them on the catwalk with feminist-slogan T-shirts, biker boots, and big matching knickers visible underneath; Carrie Bradshaw famously wore hers with a pink vest in the opening credits of *Sex and the City*. Versions on the high street abound—and luckily tend not to be transparent. You can find them in ballerina pastels or dark neutrals (the latter of which might work best for grimy city living).

The tutu's poofy, A-line shape means you need something clean and simple to wear with it on top. A medium to fine-knit jumper (think cashmere or merino wool), chunky rollneck, or long or short-sleeved T-shirt fully or half tucked in will look very elegant. You could also try it with a waisted or cropped sharp-shouldered blazer. For a tougher take, try a cropped leather jacket. It can be worn with cowboy boots, ballet pumps, heels, or even trainers.

Pencil

Straight, tight, and often formal, we tend to associate pencil skirts with corner offices. They work particularly well on straight up-and-down types and can be belted to create more of a waist. Worn with a boyfriend (note—not darted) shirt or sheer blouse and heels, they are a shortcut to polished. But keep in mind that pencils come in a variety of other materials that steer away from that trad corporate aesthetic, too. Denim takes are far more laid-back; ditto soft knitted styles. Statement versions (feather-trimmed, sequin-embellished, etc.) are great for parties. Those with a leg-flashing slit are even better.

Pleated

Pleated skirts turn up time and again on Dior catwalks. But they run the risk of looking a bit like a school uniform. I think knife pleats are the easiest to pull off and offer nice movement, particularly in satin. You could wear one of those with a softly flowing silk or sheer blouse on top, or try a waisted jacket that falls at your hip bone. A long- or short-sleeve T-shirt fully tucked in or a light-knit sweater French-tucked at the front of your waistband, with statement earrings and heels, is a lovely look for the evening.

A-line

Skirts shaped like the letter—fitted at the top and structured diagonally outward. Dior first featured this silhouette in his Spring/Summer 1955 haute couture collection, in which he paired them with slim-fitting, tailored jackets. Because the shape accentuates the waist and enhances the hips, they tend to look good on everyone and can be worn with tight- or loose-fitting tops depending on how you want to balance volume.

Tiered
& asymmetric

Tiered skirts might come with just one frilly layer at the bottom or several. The former adds an approachable bit of interest to straighter styles, while the latter is voluminous and playful. In either case, you'll be working with an asymmetric hemline—i.e., one that falls in several different places—which means the silhouette of the skirt will be doing the hard work. Once again, keep things simple on top and you won't go far wrong.

Remember that so much of getting dressed is trusting your gut—don't think that any of these styles are resolutely not for you. They can be dressed up and down, appropriated as girly or with edge. Midi skirts can be as punky as they are delicate, and both takes have been created by hands leading the creative direction at Dior.

As the man himself said on the subject of hemlines: "What is right for you is simply a matter of good taste." I have no doubt you have that already in spades.

Channel your
INNER PRINCESS

"*It is unforgivable to do what one doesn't love, especially if one succeeds.*"

Christian Dior

Palaces, galas, stables, and tiaras—how tempted are you by an old-fashioned princess fantasy? My guess would be: not very. It's not even what most working royals get to indulge in these days—you're more likely to see the Princess of Wales in a suit than a frothy ball gown, and it might not even be one with a high-end label sewn in. She often wears clothes from the high street.

If you're partial to a bit of fashion fairy tale, though—and the wardrobes of proper, rather than Disney, royalty—there is no brand more up your street than Dior. Majesty runs through its DNA.

Grace Kelly. Princess Margaret. Lady Diana. The Duchess of Sussex. Christian Dior dressed royals—and those close to—throughout his career as a couturier, and so, in turn, have his successors. Those on thrones—or in line to inherit them— flock to Dior as much today as in the debutante-centric era the label flourished in.

Study the front row at any of the brand's catwalk shows as a case in point. You are as likely to find members of modern monarchies admiring the clothes there as you are the usual fashion-industry royalty. One prince—Nikolai of Denmark— has turned his hand to modeling in a few. You can't get a more regal seal of approval than that.

It was England's spunky Princess Margaret—younger sister to Queen Elizabeth II—who started it. After enjoying a private view of the New Look collection at the Savoy Hotel in 1947, in 1951 she commissioned a bespoke Dior gown for her twenty-first birthday, which she wore to her party at Sandringham and in the Cecil Beaton-snapped official portraits to mark it.

But "gown" is not sufficient a word, really, for what Dior created for the young princess. Like everything he designed, it was nothing short of a masterpiece: a vast sensation in white silk organza and satin with a belted, boned bodice and a sequin and rhinestone embroidered skirt composed of seven—yes, seven!—layers of material. Whoa.

No surprise that Margaret went on to become a loyal client of the house. In 1954 she even acted as a guest of honor at a Dior charity fashion show hosted by the Duchess of Marl-borough at Blenheim Palace in Oxfordshire. Looks from the couturier's then new H line were modeled in aid of the British Red Cross, a moment that was revisited in May 2016 when the brand staged its Cruise 2017 show there. The models in it even followed the 1954 catwalk route.

Princess Diana was another Dior devotee. She often wore suits from the brand and in 1995 had the Lady Dior hand-bag named after her: a boxy, top-handle quilted mini tote that remains a key accessory at the label today (yours for

Christian Dior with Princess Margaret, 1951

$5,000 or more, depending what style you choose). She also attended fashion's biggest night out, New York's Met Gala, in Dior in 1996. John Galliano's navy-blue slip dress, his first creation for the house, was considered so revealing by Diana that she almost didn't wear it. But it was perfect given that the party's theme that year was in celebration of Dior.

It wasn't just the English aristocracy. There is literature devoted to Princess Grace of Monaco's relationship with Dior. Alfred Hitchcock's heroine of choice wore the brand to announce her engagement to Prince Rainier III in 1956 and continued to champion the house through the years Marc Bohan was creative director. In 1967 she cut the ribbon on the first Baby Dior store. As well as logo-branded baby accessories, it sold miniature versions of the brand's grown-up outfits—think megabucks "Mummy and me." Still does, for those in the market for a Dior bottle or pram.

Princess Charlene of Monaco; Queen Rania of Jordan; Diana's nieces Lady Amelia and Lady Eliza Spencer—the list goes on of contemporary, stately women who turn to Dior for looks that both flatter them and fit the public roles they inhabit. It's why countless celebrities choose the brand for their spotlight moments, too: Hollywood starlets from Marilyn Monroe and Elizabeth Taylor to Nicole Kidman and Jennifer Lawrence have worn Dior gowns on the red carpet and to receive awards.

All that said, it's not a surprise that a key style principle of Dior is about embracing a bit of fantasy (be it princess-leaning or not). The couturier designed clothes that allowed the wearer to step into and magnify the most glamorous parts of oneself; he thought that the right dress could transform a woman.

Embracing that idea is all about having something in your wardrobe that is a bit special. It is finding an item that changes not just how you look, but also how you feel—even if just for the night. For Dior, that meant a ball gown.

How to get that wow factor

Ball gowns are a funny thing to promote in a modern wardrobe, but there is no point skirting around the fact that Dior adored them. They were always pivotal in his collections, owing in part to the era in which he was designing (it was a ball- and gala-heavy time) but also that they, to his mind, evoked the very essence of what he believed to be feminine. Yes—the take is a little antiquated.

Park that fact for a moment. He considered the item entirely essential: it was his belief that a big fat fancy frock was as indispensable in a woman's trousseau as you might view your jeans. Dior even went as far as to suggest that a ball gown was good for one's self-esteem. Perhaps you can see his point: putting one from Dior on for the night was an opportunity to embody the most confident and bewitching version of oneself. That was his goal when he designed them, at least.

Whole narratives have been spun around the sentiment. Remade on the big screen in 2022 was *Mrs. Harris Goes to Paris*, a toothsome tale about a 1950s working-class war widow from London who buys herself a Dior gown with her dead husband's army pension and, armed with it, conquers her grief. Far-fetched? To a point, but I tend to believe that clothes can be a bit magic. Certainly, they can be transformative.

TWENTY-FIRST-CENTURY WORLD
OF HAUTE COUTURE

There are a handful of individuals on this earth for whom luxury designer made-to-measure clothing is a way of life. I'm not talking about having a tailor or owning Savile Row suits, luxuries as those are. Dior couture customers function on another sartorial level entirely. They attend specific, fanfare catwalk shows in Paris twice a year (in January and July, separate from the ready-to-wear collections shown in February and September), at which they handpick their wardrobes directly from the runway. Dior will then send its staff wherever that person may be, to conduct fittings and take measurements before creating custom pieces just for them.

You will know this if you have ever fantasized about finding—or (bravo!) found—something heart-stopping to wear to an important event, or strolled into a room, loving your outfit, with that much more spring in your step. A truly enchanting ensemble will have you walking on air. I think it is something many people experience on their wedding day—still one occasion for which investing in something bespoke is encouraged.

For Dior's haute couture customers, it is simply a way of life. These are consumers on the back of whom a big, custom-made dress will get a great deal of mileage—and not just because of how often they are flown around the world. They are the wealthiest shoppers in the world, with calendars packed full of grand events and limitless funds to spend on pieces so expensive they don't come with price tags. A ball gown makes sense in that universe. But how to take this undeniably significant item to the Dior house and make it work for the rest of us, out in the real world?

To find the answer, I think we look to the collections of Maria Grazia Chiuri. In her role as the first female creative director of Dior, she has taken the more frothy house codes and made them work in modern wardrobes. Christian Dior may have adored vast dresses for how they could make his customers look and feel, but you don't need to cosplay as a Sugar Plum Fairy to channel the principle. Below are five ways to break down that aesthetic and retool it for now.

GO BOLD ON ACCESSORIES

If you fancy wearing a tulle tutu or a frilly dress but want to dial down the girliness, consider what you wear them with. A chunky waist belt in a dark color or lug-soled shoe (be it a loafer, boot, trainer, or sandal) will toughen up fancy items and make them work in the daytime. You could also wear a plain roll-neck or T-shirt under a dress—more on which next.

CONTRAST IS KEY

Perhaps the most iconic Dior look in recent times is that of Maria Grazia Chiuri's "We Should All Be Feminists" white T-shirt paired with a sheer black maxi skirt on the Spring/Summer 2017 runway. It is a lesson in how to mix outré items with low-key pieces to create outfits that are at once elevated but also casual. See also: clean blazers over ruffled or sheer shirts, elaborate blouses or jackets with jeans, or crisp white shirts with sumptuous leather, velvet, or satin trousers or skirt.

GET ONE WOW PIECE

And it doesn't need to be a dress. A beautifully made jacket, coat, or pair of trousers that can be styled up or down and make everything else you own look better will serve you far longer than a one-off frock. Quality over quantity is key here (and something Dior himself espoused): consider spending more on something you know you will wear forever. You might even want to have something made bespoke.

PICK DARKER PALETTES

Less girly, more goth—sheer pieces in dark colors are both edgy and glamorous, at once attention-grabbing but subtle in their way, too. Many of Maria Graza Chiuri's ballerina-worthy catwalk looks at Dior come in black: it's an easy way to wear something amplified in terms of architecture and volume without it being over-powering or perhaps making you feel self-conscious.

Understated is elegant

Even the most *va-va-voom* Dior looks on its contemporary catwalks hold something back: simple jewelery, hair straight or pulled off the face, and plain accessories will keep modern fashion fairy-tale looks from tipping into OTT territory. Dior himself felt that too many ornaments could ruin a look. Simplicity is always chic.

My point in laying out these suggestions is to extract that core Dior style principle—to channel one's more confident self through extra-special items in one's wardrobe—and make it workable every day.

But, please, do not take them as rote. Dior was a stickler for individuality and he encouraged his clients not to follow trends. The point of channeling your inner princess is not to dress up as something you are not. It's purely about feeling fab.

Paint from the
COUTURIER'S
PALETTE

"*Midnight blue is the only color that can ever compete with black.*"

Christian Dior

We mentioned in chapter one that architecture was important to Dior. Of all the objects of beauty he was passionate about—and there were many, from flowers to the way his immaculate female models or "mannequins" walked, to fine art—buildings held special prominence. He fancied himself an architect at one point in his life, and you can see that inclination in the technical tailoring of his designs and his obsession with silhouette.

But it was not just the structure of Dior's haute couture pieces that were influenced by the real estate he most admired. The color palette he drew from was, too.

An elegant Anglo-Norman villa atop a cliff in Normandy. A neoclassical hôtel particulier in the 8th arrondissement of

Paris. There are two buildings which embody Dior's color palette and appear to have influenced what shades he turned to over and over in his collections. Said structures are not, suffice it to say, your average piles. The first is his former family home in Granville: a manor house named Les Rhumbs, with expansive views over the sea. The second is still the beating heart of the brand today: Christian Dior's four-story *grand dame* headquarters at 30 Avenue Montaigne.

It is the exterior of the former that shows us what two hues Dior adored and which are still house codes now. Pink and gray have been described by the designer as his best-loved colors in couture; he used them when designing his clothes but also his atelier, home, accessories, beauty products, and, well, anything else with the Christian Dior label attached.

They are also the colors of his youth, for they are the colors that Les Rhumbs was constructed of. The pretty home, now a museum dedicated to the designer, is a work of pale pink pebble dash that stood on a foundation of gray gravel. The common mist and mizzle of the Normandy landscape it stands against is equally silvery—ditto the clifftop it is set on. Both of these act as a stark contrast to the rose-hued plaster of the villa and the actual roses in its garden, which Dior would often sit among with his mother and sketch. It's no surprise that these colors held a certain romance for the designer—for the first five years of his life, he was surrounded by them.

One perhaps doesn't have to take a great leap to associate pink with Dior. That a house built on trad femininity should have strong links to an unapologetically camp shade makes sense. To many, it might feel a tad obvious. But Dior was truly fond of it. Per his 1954 *Little Dictionary of Fashion*, he thought pink the "sweetest of all the colours" and that everyone should own at least one item in the shade in their wardrobe. Think on that for a minute. Do you?

Personally, I like pink. And when I think of Dior, it is one of the shades that springs to mind. Natalie Portman has much to do with that. I recall her 2013 television ad campaign for the Miss Dior perfume, appropriately named *La Vie en Rose*, was a celebration of the shade. In it, she wears pink clothes, is shot against pink backgrounds through what looks like a warm, rose-tinted lens, and lies on a bed of pink buds. No prizes for guessing the color of Miss Dior itself. It is the brand's first and most famous perfume—we will return to it in chapter ten.

I remember a shoot from that year, too. In *British Vogue*'s September 2013 issue, Cara Delevingne, the then fledgling supermodel, was shot in Dior for a twelve-page, pink-themed editorial that still captivates me. Nestled among the back-to-back blushing looks styled by Francesca Burns was a sleek, candy-floss-hued mid-length coat dress. It had a sheer, darker pink panel across the décolletage and a chic, flared-out hem—the work of Raf Simons for Dior. I haven't forgotten it—in fact, I think I went out to try and find my own affordable version of it. Great fashion sticks.

You can see gray everywhere at Dior, too—once you look for it. The color has been present at the brand from its very foundations. The couturier himself elevated the most muted of neutrals in 1946 when he chose to paint the salon walls of his label's new digs in the shade. Thirty Avenue Montaigne, a private mansion originally built in 1865 by Napoleon's son, was chosen by Dior for its chic façade, desirable location and what he described as "manageable proportions." Today, it's been expanded a touch: as well as still acting as the brand's global flagship, it has a museum, restaurant, and apartment for overnight stays.

In 1946, it was intended to act as a blank canvas for Dior's collections. He wanted to paint the walls of his salon a color that would not detract or distract. Black would not do (too dark), neither would white (too simple). And so, with the help of his contemporary Victor Grandpierre—a fashion photographer-cum-decorator—he plumped for a soft, pearly gray.

This was in keeping with his overall Louis XVI-inspired aesthetic vision for the house. Dior wanted to update and reinvigorate the interiors trend that had been all the rage in the years he spent in Paris as a child. This was achieved with those melting gray walls but also with white accents, crystal chandeliers, draped toile de Jouy, and branded hat boxes scattered in a casual—but, have no doubt, painstakingly curated—manner. It would have been Pinterest heaven.

That gray is now known as Dior gray (at least, it is in high-fashion circles). It is the color of the boxes Dior products come in and of the paneled exterior of many Dior stores around the world. You can buy handbags, tailoring, and trainers in it; it has even been reimagined by the house as a unisex scent and candle.

To Dior, gray was the most elegant neutral on the color wheel. It was his view that you could wear it with anything; that it suited everyone in its various shades. He found it to be complex; not just the murky in-between mix of black and white, but a tone to be celebrated all on its own. There is no doubt he thought it especially nice with pink, but there were a few other colors he was keen on, too. Blue, red, and black all meant something to the designer. Below is a guide to the couturier's essential palette and tips on making the shades work for you.

Find your shade

We know by now that a key style principle of Dior's is to ignore trends and diktats in favor of finding what suits each individual best. That, of course, applies to color. You can see it filter through in the designer's own musings on various shades—there is never *not* a note on complexion or even personality type when he discusses his favorite hues and on whom they might be best worn. This is no surprise for a man who lived and breathed fashion: he even named his couture looks as though they were his children. They were as alive to him as anything else. So of course colors had character to him, too.

We do not have to take such an anthropological approach. But we can take a scientific one. It's true that colors will complement us in different ways. That is very much down to skin undertone. Whether yours is cool, warm, olive, or neutral can be determined using an easy test with a white piece of paper. You can find out how to do it on the opposite page.

THE PAPER TEST

In a naturally lit area, take a piece of white paper in front of a mirror and place it next to your face. If your skin looks pinkish, you have **cool** undertones. If it looks yellow, you have **warm**. If it's green you see, you have **olive** undertones. Those who see nothing are **neutral** (good news—you can wear pretty much anything).

Black

Dior adored delicate shades, but he was also keen on the power of contrast (his New Look Le Bar suit, with white jacket and black skirt, is just one example). Black, he felt—as many do—was flattering on everyone. He saw it as striking and useful on every occasion: easy to wear and a shortcut to chic. He thought that an LBD was something every woman should have in her wardrobe. It's a philosophy that has proved timeless—and hard to argue with. It doesn't matter what your skin tone is; anyone can wear black.

Blue

Two shades of blue are often used at Dior—a pale shade in line with the couturier's Louis XVI leanings and dependable navy. Pale blue is delicate and pretty, and will suit those with cool undertones and blue eyes. On navy, I could wax lyrical. There is a reason fashion editors love it. A navy jumper is probably the most-seen item on journalists at Fashion Week, a navy blazer the most useful item anyone can own. Really. Dior agrees—he proclaimed navy to have the same useful qualities as black. It suits everyone.

Pink

How much pink is in your wardrobe? You might own one piece, per Dior's rule, but it could well be confined to your underwear drawer. Pink comes with all kinds of connotations that can put off anyone who doesn't want to look overly girly. I think one way to approach the more saccharine, pale iterations (great for cool undertones) is by finding contrastingly mannish items in them: a silk shirt, cashmere sweater, or even boxy outerwear—perhaps a double-breasted peacoat. A Breton-striped long-sleeve T-shirt in the shade would feel contemporary and cool, without being too sweet. Bolder takes—fuschia, say—might be easier to carry as pops of color on accessories: a shoe, handbag, scarf, or hat. Don't let me stop you from wearing it head to toe if you want to; Dior would be all for it.

Red

Dior saved red for his boldest evening wear
and he featured it in every collection, often
as the final statement look—what he referred
to as his "*coup de* Trafalgar." He thought red
was a color worth showing off, for it was
a shade that denoted fire and passion.
There is a red for every undertone (ditto a
red lipstick). Cool undertones look great
in pink- or blue-based shades; neutrals
can work orangey reds and mauves. Warm
undertones suit brick, cherry, or rust; those
with olive tones might like yellow- or orange-
based reds. Dior liked bright reds best—he
thought they suited frocks, accessories for more
muted outfits, or, in winter, coats. Festive!

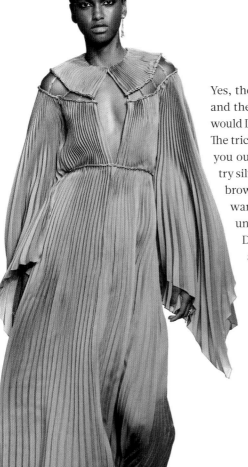

Gray

Yes, there are different shades of gray—and there is one for everyone. Why else would Dior have been so obsessed with it? The trick is finding a hue that won't wash you out. Cool undertones may want to try silver-, blue-, or violet-based grays; brown- and green-based shades suit warm undertones. Olive and neutral undertones can pull off most shades. Dior thought the color was best accented by white and I agree—a gray sweater and white jeans is one of my favourite looks. I warm it up with gold jewelery.

I have not gone into every color on the chart here because it was Dior's view that the basics of every wardrobe should be built on shades that are easy to wear. He believed that you'd get far more wear out of a classic or neutrally toned dress than you would one in a trendy color of the moment.

With that in mind, he encouraged his clients to bring color into their ensembles via accessories. He thought said accents could be used to change the look of clothes you already had. This is a timely lesson for now, when the world needs to move away from seasonal, trend-led fast fashion and buy timeless, good-quality clothes they can wear, wear, repair, and rewear.

One final note on the topic. Dior felt that two colors in any outfit would be sufficient; ditto two accessories in the same color. Wearing a hat, bag, belt, and shoes in the same matching vibrant shade? Disaster— by Dior standards, anyway.

7

Step into a
STILETTO

"You can never take too much care over the choice of your shoes."

Christian Dior

Fair warning: whatever you think of Dior might be about to change. Although, that rather depends on your philosophy on footwear. If you are someone who is partial to a sandal or pump with a tall spike attached, then good news: you and Dior are kindred spirits.

If, however, you (like me) would rather wear literally anything else on your feet, I regret to inform you that the couturier's approach to footwear will rub. Dior loved heels. He actually thought flats were suitable for just two activities: playing sports or visiting the countryside. Not only that, but the most prominent shoe designer he worked with practically invented *the* heel. Yes, I am indeed, talking about the stiletto.

Wincing? Look, I know. It's not the news I wanted to deliver either. My love of a walkable heel aside, it feeds into that old trope in high fashion that beauty is pain (not even something the glossiest magazine fashion editor would tout now). Be that as it may, stilettos supported the arch of Dior's New Look. Pity those of his poor catwalking mannequins; they were nearly always in court shoes when modeling at 30 Avenue Montaigne. Those pumps, with a low-cut upper, pointed toe, and mid to high heels, were Dior's favorite shoe. He thought they went with everything. He liked the way the heel of them made his clients walk: elegantly, to his mind, with a swing in their step. He liked how they made feet look narrower (preferred), and, most of all, he liked how courts departed from the flats, blocky mid-heels, and wedges that had become fashionable during the war. He was designing for a new era after all—his was a New Look. Any shoe bearing the Dior name or designed to be worn with Dior haute couture had to live up to it.

Dior worked with a number of shoe designers before he found the right foot for his glass slipper, as it were. You probably haven't heard of Georges Mad, David Evins, and André Perugia—but what about Roger Vivier? It was he who, in 1953, began a professional relationship with Dior that would outlast the couturier's life. Together, the pair changed what women wore on their feet—not just then, but forever after.

If you have to ask why, look at any of the basic heels sold at designer and high-street brands alike. My bet is there will be a black or nude stiletto pump in there. That heel's original name, coined by Vivier, was the *Aiguille*—and at the time he designed it, it was new: sharper, taller, and slightly more curved than what had come before. It, in Vivier's own words, "traced a silhouette with a single stroke," changing the way its wearer walked and held themselves. Per the words of shoe historians, it began a footwear revolution.

Roger Vivier

The French shoe designer Roger Vivier—whose shoes are recognizable within the style set for their architectural heels and crystal buckle adornments—had been a sculpture student before he turned his hand to shoemaking. No surprise he and Dior, the architecture-head, hit it off. After a few meetings over dinner, the pair set out a five-year contract under which Vivier would design two shoe collections for Dior per year, plus any made-to-measure footwear, a plan that fulfilled Dior's wish that his clients be dressed in the brand from head to toe. Vivier remained at Dior for ten years in all, creating masterpiece pumps for Yves Saint Laurent and Marc Bohan, too, before setting up shop on his own. He died in 1998 but the label lives on.

I am wary of claiming that it was entirely the invention of Vivier, though. Several shoe designers of that era are credited with the development of the stiletto as we know it today, from Salvatore Ferragamo (Marilyn Monroe's favorite) to Charles Jourdan. What we do know is that it was Vivier who took it to new heights in his posting at Dior. His sculpted needle heels came with reinforcing steel rods in them, a pioneering technical feat that allowed even the skinniest iterations to bear more weight. Their impact on women's footwear cannot be overstated (nor on their podiatrist bills).

A glance back over that era of Dior footwear is enough to make you believe that any discomfort sustained wearing the label's shoes was worth it. Dior and Vivier's pumps were nothing short of *haute foot-ure*. Together, they took the humble court shoe and elevated it to unprecedented levels of glamour.

No expense was spared on the materials or embellishments, no boundary untested on the techniques. Under Vivier, a pair of shoes from Dior was as exquisite as any item of the brand's clothes. Forget practical—they were downright precious. I am surprised anyone actually wore them, for they look more suited to life atop a silk pillow, behind glass.

Beads, pearls, feathers, and exotic leathers. Embroidered silk-satin and Chantilly lace. None of it sounds suitable to grace a 1950s pavement, but Vivier's Dior shoes were not designed to walk miles in. Rather, it was about how you walked in them. Dior had opinions on posture and gait—he thought a beautiful outfit was wasted on anyone who slouched.

A heel of just the right height, he thought, could bring that along—help his clients walk more elegantly, with grace. It's a theory that doesn't quite land today. Certainly not since the dawn of nightclubs—the most glamorous of which heels might be worn into, but tend to be defeatedly hand-carried out of.

However you feel about heels, there is a Dior shoe principle to fit everyone. Above all, that is because Dior—as with all things fashion—cared deeply about them. The shoes, I mean. There was never too much time one could spend, he thought, on picking a pair out. To his mind, they were an indicator of taste and elegance. That might sound dramatic, but his point was that they should not be an afterthought. What you wear on your feet matters.

Shopping for shoes

The Dior take on filling one's wardrobe was absolutely quality over quantity. He espoused the power of well-made, classic items that one could wear again and again.

So, when shoe shopping—for whichever style you like—consider the three key details on the next page.

What are they made of?

Look for high-quality materials. It doesn't have to be leather or suede, though Dior was a fan of those. Lots of "vegan" leather has the look and feel of the real stuff and wears just as well.

How much do they cost?

Fast-fashion stores are full of bargains, but ask yourself how long a pair of shoes from there will last. Saving up for a slightly more expensive style that you can repair and rewear will save you money (and help the planet) in the long run.

What color are they?

Dior liked black, white, navy, and brown for footwear; I personally get tons of wear out of flats in green, red, and gold. Whatever the shade of the shoe you are thinking of buying, think about how well it will work with the rest of your wardrobe. If it's only going to look good with a few outfits—and unless it is for a specific special occasion that demands it—perhaps that pair isn't for you.

I have some other sage advice for shoe shopping: **never buy the pair that are uncomfortable on the first wear.** As someone with large feet (a UK 9), I spent years trying to squish my feet into styles I loved that weren't quite right, in the hope they would stretch. I have bought heels I could never walk in and designer pairs I didn't truly love in sample sales just because of the label stamped in the sole. Each pair ended up costing me in the long run—not just because I barely wore them, but in the price of blister plasters.

Keep them polished

How you care for your shoes matters, too. You probably don't need me to tell you that Dior would not have approved of scuffed toes (easy enough to avoid if you are a haute couture client getting whisked around by chauffeur).

For the rest of us pavement pounders, **a local cobbler** can help you take care of your favorite shoes for little cost, whether that's repainting leather or replacing soles.

It is also worth **investing in products you can use at home**: suede protector, leather cleaner, etc.

High-end restoration services are also abundant now, but be warned: their repairs might cost more than the price of a pair of new shoes.

The ultimate Dior shoe

As to what constitutes a Dior shoe, a glance at the brand's website today would suggest that any model works. The modern Dior customer is certainly not confined to heels: the label stocks espadrilles, block-heeled pumps, loafers, trainers, boots, and flat or chunky sandals. Referring to the aforementioned guidance in choosing versions of your own won't lead you far wrong.

However, there is one shoe in particular that stands out for its preeminence in brand collections from its early days. I want to highlight it because it is one, to my mind, that works in every wardrobe and speaks to both Christian Dior's leanings *and* also the needs of your average consumer. It is **the slitten** (that's a slingback kitten heel). If you are going to invest in one surefire Dior shoe, this is it.

Of course, the brand doesn't call them that. Today, the style is known as the J'Adior Slingback Pump. It comes in every color and print you can think of, with a sharply pointed toe, a slim curved heel at either 2.5 inches or 4 inches, and a branded embroidered ribbon for the heel strap. You'd be hard pushed to attend Fashion Week and not spot a pair: today, they are a cult item.

Jeans and a nice top. Midi or miniskirts. Frocks of all kinds. Suits. There's not much that a pair of slittens doesn't pair well with. They are at once refined and sexy, timeless but contemporary. You can buy brilliant versions at all price points and find a pair with a heel height that works for you. Plain or printed iterations fit the bill—ditto those in satin, leather, or suede. Any will take you from day- to nighttime easily. To my mind, they are actually the perfect shoe.

A FINAL FOOTNOTE

Don't feel like every pair of shoes you buy has to be simple or classic. I was surprised to read Dior's advice on footwear, given how extraordinary Vivier's pump designs were. With that in mind, I believe it is just as fitting with the couturier's approach to have one pair that is truly fabulous, just as you might a dress or suit. Vivier's designs were always ornate—and shoes embroidered with toile de Jouy, floral, and seasonal motifs are mainstays at the brand today.

In short: there is nothing
wrong with having one
showstopper shoe for special
occasions—even if it means
traveling by taxi while they are
on your feet.

Grab a grown–up
BAG

> "Don't buy much
> but make sure that
> what you buy
> is good."

Christian Dior

Microbags the size of a Tic Tac (Jacquemus, 2019). Metal and leather woven supermarket shopping baskets (Chanel, 2014). Clutches shaped like a pigeon (JW Anderson, 2022) and bin-bag-inspired black holdalls (Balenciaga, 2022).

Forget global arbiters of taste: the average shopper might wonder what planet luxury fashion designers have been on for the last decade, based on what they have labeled a handbag. The truth is that, since the dawn of Instagram, what constitutes an It-cessory has changed. No longer does the 0.01-percent consumer necessarily want something in a classic shape or timeless color (which, to be frank, they probably already have). In the economy of likes and shares, outré is in—and it is the internet, as much as fashion editors, which gives a handbag cult status.

The examples listed above are a case in point. Brands have labeled them playful; among influencers they have become must-haves. They have, between them, launched a thousand memes and sent Twitter into meltdown over their price tags. By doing so they have achieved their goal: to break the internet as well as sales quotas. Whether these bags are dreamed up out of humor is of no consequence, because it is brands that have the last laugh: accessories are the financial backbone of big fashion houses and these items are cash cows. I mean it: that JW Anderson plastic pigeon was sold out more often than not.

Not all brands buy into this. Nor, in fact, do most fashion editors. They prefer something stealth, well made, and functional—perhaps only recognizable for what it is to those who really know. If they are going to invest in a designer handbag, you can, nine times out of ten, bet your bottom dollar it will be in black, brown, white, red, or navy. It will be of a design that will work in their wardrobe season after season and of which they are unlikely to get bored. Anything more OTT can be easily hired from rental platforms now. In my experience, you don't want those for longer than a week anyway.

I'm telling you all this because Dior does not, by and large, buy into zany, look-at-me Insta-cessories. It is also a brand whose classic handbags are still sacrosanct in fashion circles, in that they remain both desired and admired. You will know what I am talking about if you have ever mooned over the brand's website or paused at one of its store windows. Dior makes bags that are—while, yes, mighty pricey—decidedly grown-up. They are polished, made in good sizes, and enchanting for the reason that you could see how they would fit into and work in your own life. They come in seasonal colors and prints—they have to keep the regular customers coming back—but were each originally designed in plain black or the brand's navy logo print. Put succinctly: they are sensible.

Dior's wish for handbags bearing his name was always thus. Like everything he put his hand to, a clutch, shoulder bag, or purse by Christian Dior had—and still has—to be two things: made of the very best materials on the one hand and crafted in a distinctly sophisticated silhouette on the other. To him, the simplest designs in the finest-quality leather or textiles always beat out anything trend-led or cheaply made. He also thought his handbags should have a place for everything in them—a given, you'd think, but not always.

In my opinion, there are four handbags that are synonymous with the House of Dior. None were actually designed by the man himself. While, yes, accessories were available during his tenure as head of the brand, the House of Dior was not a leather-goods producer, and thus any seasonal accessories were licensed out. They were also designed to be worn as part of a head-to-toe Dior look; something to be added on to a clothing order. They were not the one-off purchases Dior customers visit its stores for today.

It was down to the couturier's successors, then, to define Dior's handbag status on the world stage. Accessories became even more important to luxury houses long after Dior's death—it was, over time, understood by accountants that while not everyone could afford haute couture, they might be able to spring for something smaller. It was an astute realization that launched mainline handbag models at high-end fashion labels all over the world.

Dior's have been carried by royalty, on the red carpet, front row at Fashion Week, and by chic men and women everywhere else besides. Below are the four key styles to know—and the characteristics to take note of when shopping for your own version.

1

Lady Dior

The story goes that the Lady Dior was initially created in 1995 not to be mass-produced, but especially for Princess Diana. Bernadette Chirac, France's first lady, had approached the house ahead of the British royal's official visit to Paris, wishing that the label's then creative director Gianfranco Ferré would make something just for her. No one expected what happened next: Diana wore the bag so much, it was renamed "Princesse" and sold 200,000 units over the subsequent two years. Commonly called Dior's first It-bag, the square, padded, top-handle bag became a house code and now comes in several sizes and seasonal finishes.

Shape
square

Size
small

**How
to carry**
by hand

Finish
topstitch quilting
with gold or silver
charm hardware

Size
medium

Shape
like the name—in
a curved saddle

**How
to carry**
on the shoulder

Finish
matte leather or
logo embroidery
with gold hardware

2

The Saddle

John Galliano is the man behind Dior's iconic Saddle, debuting it as part of Dior's Spring 2000 ready-to-wear collection in 1999. It quickly gained traction as Carrie Bradshaw's favorite handbag (she wore it in the third episode of *Sex and the City*'s fifth season) and later on other aspirational noughties sitcoms: *The O.C.* and *The Simple Life*, to wit. The logo-leaden motif it initially came in was actually the work of Marc Bohan; he designed Dior's "Oblique" print—the repetitive, stacked, diagonal "DIOR" pattern—in 1967 during his post as creative director. Maria Grazia Chiuri brought the Saddle back in 2018, this time in sleek leathers and embroidery. It comes in a whole spectrum of variations today.

3

The Book Tote

A contemporary icon, the Dior Book Tote arrived under Maria Grazia Chiuri as part of her Spring 2018 collection. It has been selling and selling ever since. The open carryall (it has no closing fastening), said to be based on a sketch by Marc Bohan from 1967, is beloved by the busy, multitasking, and jet-setting for its roomy practicality, ritzy designs, and the fact it can be personalized.

Size
large

Shape
rectangle

How to carry
by hand, or fashion-editor style: atop your carry-on suitcase when traveling

CHRISTIAN DIOR
PARIS

Finish
embroidered fabric

145

Shape
boxy

Size
medium

Finish
glossy leather
with gold
hardware

**How
to carry**
over the shoulder,
cross body, or by
hand—the strap is
adjustable

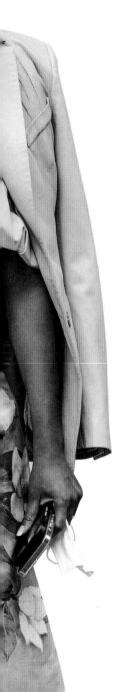

4

The 30 Montaigne

Dior's 30 Montaigne is another new design that has quickly gained cult status. The boxy, slim, calfskin flap bag with a "CD" gold buckle was introduced in 2021 as part of the brand's new collection of the same name, which was designed to represent staple emblems of the house: the Bar jacket, timeless knitwear, wear-anywhere separates, and essential accessories.

Now you know the bags, there are a few rules. Dior was exacting on how one should carry, treat, and style a handbag. I have broken them down into five lessons on the opposite page.

1
Find the right size.
Dior thought that the right
handbag should have
a place for everything.

2
Differ by day and night.
You could change the look and feel
of the same outfit by switching
your bag up, per the couturier's
opinion. He suggested simple,
classic styles for day and smaller
embroidered or embellished
iterations for evening.

3
Choose a distinct shape.
Boxy, curved, or something
else altogether, your handbag
should have a clean, elegant
silhouette. Think square,
rectangle, half-moon, circular,
or something even more
distinct, à la Saddle.

4
Look after it.
Treat your handbags as Dior
suggests you do your shoes—
with love and care. Good-quality
material lasts forever if you are
prudent with it. Keeping your
accessories in dust bags and out
of the light is the easiest way
to avoid wear and tear.

5
Don't overstuff it.
What's in the bottom of your
bag? If you can count spare loose
change, pens without lids, and
random pieces of chewing gum,
Dior would have a stern word to
say to you. In his *Little Dictionary
of Fashion*, he advised not to use
a handbag like an extra rubbish
bin, lest it lose its shape.

Above all, find yourself a bag that looks and feels grown-up. A Dior handbag adds polish to any outfit. It is distinctive for the fact it is refined. One in his style should be take-anywhere and ever-after: yours to wear anytime with anything, again and again. Just remember to empty out the spare change and dry-cleaning receipts once in a while. Debris was not approved by Dior.

Go for GOLD

"*Color is what gives jewels their worth. They light up and enhance the face.*"

Christian Dior

Dior was a designer who was big on the little. From buttons and pleating to embroidery and stitching—not to mention the addition of a belt, bag, hat, or pair of gloves—details, to his mind, mattered. In the balance of his outfits, they held as great a weight as anything else and thus, in his atelier, there was no finishing touch left unconsidered. Every flourish was treated with the greatest gravity. Anything less was considered equal to not bothering at all.

It conjures a scene often painted in pop-culture send-ups of fashion types: a group of immaculate, highly strung individuals arguing dramatically over two earrings or shades of blue that, to the untrained eye, look exactly the same. I suspect there have been several such moments over the years at

30 Avenue Montaigne. And while it might seem obsessive—
perhaps pointlessly so—to some, this painstaking rumination
is what sets the great fashion designers apart. Dior cared
deeply about his clothes, clients, and everything else that
contributed to each of his collections' overall look. Getting
the season's aesthetic just so—and every element of it, big
or small—required a laser eye. Nothing escaped his focus.

Naturally, he didn't miss the shiniest details of all. Dior
was not a jewelery designer but—surprise!—on the topic,
he had thoughts. He licensed jewelery to be shown with his
haute couture as early as 1948 and those gem pieces, like his
clothes, had to be a departure from everything else on the
market. Jewelery through the 1940s had been chunky, so
Dior's was dainty. Coco Chanel's reign of power among the
style set in wartime had popularized fake statement gems;

he espoused the value of the real thing. And the motifs he turned to again and again were undeniably soft and graceful: delicate bows and flowers.

The house worked with several different jewelery designers, but it was a collaboration with Swarovski that is still famed today. In 1956—just a year before Dior's death—he and Manfred Swarovski began working together on a bespoke stone that would embody the couturier's singular vision. The result was the "Aurora Borealis"—a shimmering, multifaceted crystal named after the Northern Lights, which reflected multiple colors. It proved a phenomenon. Dior used it for jewelery but also for embroidery on his ball gowns, its mirroring effect making it a fine match for an entire spectrum of colors. You may have seen one in the flesh and not realized—it is still used by designers today.

Jewelery is a much larger piece of the Dior brand puzzle now. It has its own creative director, individual collections, and status as a sizable contributor to the house's profit margin. It makes both fine creations and fakes (costume pieces it labels "fashion jewelery")—all elegant and refined bijoux that are inspired by the brand's core codes. They are playful, delicate, and eye-catching. Unfortunately, the price tags they come with are not quite as small-scale.

No matter. You don't need to buy Dior jewelery to emulate its aesthetic. You just need to know what attributes to look for in your own trinkets—and how to wear them.

Adorn yourself

Dior was quite plain in his views on jewelery. He had preferences on precious metals, motifs, and any earring, necklace, or bracelet's modes of styling. That's good news for us—it makes breaking down his approach easy.

GO FOR GOLD

The first thing to know is how Dior felt about gold. He loved it. The metallic fascinated him: he used it generously in couture and later it influenced perfumes and cosmetics, too. So it makes sense that the most basic jewelery principle is: **go for gold**. Choosing an ornament for your neck, earlobe, or wrist in that yellow metal is the easiest way to channel Dior. Yes, more than silver, I'm afraid.

Now, that might make you shudder. Jewelery is personal and I am conscious that the metal we wear reflects that: whether we are a gold or silver person, as it were, is as much a characteristic as our hair or eye color. As a rule of thumb, gold jewelery tends to flatter warm skin undertones and silver creations cool. But skin tone aside, you may just not like yellow gold. For you, I have a cheat.

There's not just one type of gold. Dior may have preferred the sunshine-yellow shade, but there are rose and white creations, too. The former, that of a burnished pinkish hue, suits everyone and is very pretty. The latter looks just like silver. Told you it was cheating.

GET LUCKY

Now you've got your metal sorted, what sort of bijoux did Dior like most? Charming ones, of course. No—literally. The couturier was fascinated by lucky charms—

symbols that had divine or talismanic qualities—and that has fed into the house's jewelery collections old and new. The same motifs recur. That's why the second lesson on the topic of trinkets is to **get lucky**. Jewelery that incorporates bows, flowers, stars, or four-leaf clovers is very Dior. You might even like to get yourself a charm bracelet so that you can wear them all at once.

Stars and flowers are significant in particular. Flowers in Dior jewelery speak to what the vintage jewelery expert Susan Caplan, who sources and sells original Dior jewelery from across every era, calls Dior's "romanticism." Well, we know the man had those leanings. It's his devotion to stars that is a little more woo-woo.

Dior did not turn his nose up at divination or superstition; he once said that the biggest factor of his life was his own good luck—and he took any symbols of good fortune terribly seriously. So when, strolling down the Rue du Faubourg Saint Honoré in 1946 and on the cusp of launching his brand, he stumbled upon a gold metal star that had fallen from a horse-drawn carriage, he took it as a sign. It is one that has been showing up across Dior creations ever since—even on its gift packaging.

GET REAL

Now to the most important bit—the sparkle. Dior was a fan of frosting, but the fact is that when it came to gemstones, he preferred them small—and ideally real. He didn't think that a whacking great diamond was an indicator of taste, more so just one's bank balance. That was doubly applicable to any oversized costume jewelry. Fakes were fine by him, but he thought that less was more.

It goes back to a recurring theme in this book: quality over quantity. Dior thought it better to have less flashy jewelery in finer materials than a look-at-me imposter. It's why the final principle is to **get real**. But don't let that put you off. I'm not about to suggest you buy your next pair of earrings in the Diamond District.

That's one option, of course—and there is every reason to have one or two special trinkets in your arsenal. Whether as a gift from someone or to yourself, fine jewelery is often used to mark special occasions and milestones. If you don't know where to start, try a stud earring—or pair of—in your gemstone of choice or a solitaire necklace or bracelet: that's a single jewel on a fine chain. Nothing would be more Dior—these

pieces are delicate, the most refined bit of sparkle. Perfection.

But this is not the 1950s. You don't need to go to a diamond dealer or designer store for the genuine article: today we have access to a multitude of demi-fine jewelery brands who offer a middle ground between high end and the high street. They tend to use stones in a lower carat or plated precious metals, which give the effect of the real thing without the monster price tags.

You'll pay a little more to shop demi-fine than at fast-fashion brands, but that is rather fitting with Dior's diktat. If you can save up to invest in better-quality items, it will be worth it, not just because they will last and last but because they won't leave that telltale green hue wherever they have been resting. You know the one I mean.

A final note on styling: do it your way. We know Dior was a fan of individuality, and that applies to wearing jewelery. You should use your trinkets to express yourself. They are your most subtle and useful tool to be playful in even the most low-key or formal outfits. So adopt these principles how you see fit. The gems should shine, but in them, so should your personality.

10

Fresh, floral, and
FABULOUS

"A woman's perfume tells more about her than her handwriting."

Christian Dior

And so, to the finishing touches—for we know our couturier's style principles are certainly not limited to your wardrobe. Anyone who has wandered through the beauty-concessions hall of a department store will see that: Dior is a giant of the beauty industry, its products oozing every bit as much glamour as any of its clothing or accessories.

Those products are just as, if not even more, important to the brand's business model. They offer the same indulgence and promise of transformation as everything else it sells—but at what, for most people, is a more achievable price point. In that way Dior's cosmetics, fragrances, and skincare are a gateway to the gilded world of high fashion; a small piece of the brand that anyone can take home. Think about it: the aver-

age consumer may not be able to stretch to a Dior handbag—but they probably can afford one of its Addict lipsticks.

With that in mind, the modern-day scale of Dior fragrance and beauty is no surprise; it is a label that hundreds of thousands want to possess their own part of. No wonder that at the end of 2021, the value of cosmetics and fragrances sold by the house came to 7.11 billion dollars. But you can trace its potential back to day one. Because, yes, the House of Christian Dior began with a man and a dream and a dove-gray salon in Paris and a New Look. But it also began with a scent—that of Miss Dior.

Perhaps you have a bottle of the rose-pink perfume at home. Chances are you know someone who does—Miss Dior launched officially in December 1947 and is still hotly coveted today.

The scent has been a hit since the very first moment it encountered the noses of Dior's clientele, just as they crossed the threshold of the salon at 30 Avenue Montaigne. The couturier had planned it thus: he had commissioned a perfume that "smells of love" to accompany his first collection—something that would reflect the new romantic mood he hoped his haute couture would usher in. It was duly spritzed about the *maison*, on the mannequins and salon drapes, with the intention of suggesting that, at Dior, one could find novelty in every sense. Quite literally.

Dior now has several famous fragrances—J'adore and Poison to name just two—but it is the story attached to Miss Dior that is truly fascinating. That is less because of the perfume itself and more to do with who it is named after. Miss Dior was a real person, you see. Her name was Catherine, also known as Caro, Dior, and she was the youngest—and favorite—sister of Christian.

She was a lot more than just that, though. She was a resistance fighter during World War II, a cause she joined in

1941. Three years later she became a Gestapo prisoner and torture victim. Then, after failing to comply by giving away information about her comrades, she became an inmate at concentration camps: Ravensbrück, Torgau, Abteroda, and lastly, in 1945, Markkleeberg. Against all odds, she made it out alive and went on to live a quiet life devoted to her garden and, following her brother's death in 1957, preserving his artistic legacy.

Like Miss Dior herself, the fragrance is complex. It is made with roses grown from a field at La Colle Noire, the estate Christian Dior purchased in 1951, and has notes of lily of the valley and peony. And it is definitive of how important fragrance was to Dior in general; he thought everyone should have a signature scent and, in 1949, even created a dress inspired by his first perfume: a strapless gown covered in silk flowers. To him, the beauty and craftsmanship of a perfume and that of haute couture were not just comparable. They went hand in hand.

Poetic indeed. But the same enthusiasm applied to all matters of grooming where Dior was concerned. The couturier was profusive on the topic and had ideas on how to be neat and tidy from head to toe. It's not as high maintenance as it sounds—promise. Let's begin with your nails.

Nails

How much do you think about your nails? Perhaps you are a manicure addict; maybe you never think about them at all. You could, like me, be guilty of biting them—or your job or sport requires that you keep them short.

Whatever sort of nail person you are, the fact is that Dior would have preferred them neat. He thought that good grooming was the cornerstone of elegance and that a fabulous outfit would be let down by a chipped nail.

While that sounds bossy, I see his point. A manicure is a fast track to looking polished. But you don't have to go to a nail bar to get one. You don't even have to use colored paint (I'd actually recommend against it if you are worried about upkeep).

Juanita Huber-Millet, founder and creative director at the British nail-salon chain Townhouse, has kindly put together a DIY guide for you to try at home. Your hands and feet will thank her for it—as will your bank balance.

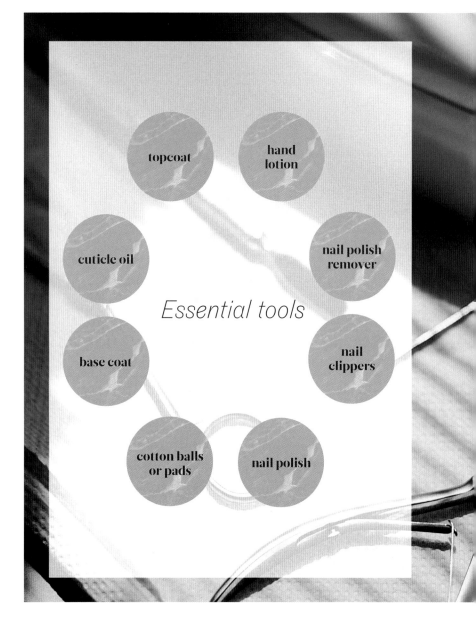

topcoat

hand lotion

cuticle oil

nail polish remover

Essential tools

base coat

nail clippers

cotton balls or pads

nail polish

Step-by-step

●

File your nails to the desired shape and length—
if you can't decide, opt for a "squoval" (square with
rounded edges), as this suits all nail lengths. To
avoid any damage, file them in one direction.

●

Apply a base coat to your nails and let them dry
completely.

●

Apply one or two even coats of your desired nail
polish. Wait for each coat to dry before applying the
next.

●

Next, use a cotton bud dipped in nail polish
remover to clean up any mistakes or polish left on
your skin.

●

Once all polish is dry, add a topcoat.

●

The most important step is moisture, moisture,
moisture—invest in cuticle oil and a rich hand
cream to keep your nails looking their best.

Hair

Dior had one rule for hair: make it manageable. He thought the best hairstyles were those that could be achieved easily at home. That's got less to do with how handy you are with a pair of tongs and more about keeping your hair in good condition. It also relies on you having a brilliant cut—a style that will work harder than you want to at styling it.

Fashion's favorite hairdresser George Northwood—who has snipped split ends off the heads of Alexa Chung, Rosie Huntington-Whiteley, and Daisy Edgar-Jones—is an expert in this. His so-called "undone" haircuts get better and better as they grow out and are in hot demand on a daily basis in his two London salons.

First, he says don't be afraid to spend money on your hairdresser. "When I was young, my mother would have her hair cut and it would never look as good as the day she walked out of the salon," he says. "Investing in a good haircut and color goes a long way. I'd almost leave it longer between appointments than compromising on quality."

I tend to agree. You wear your hair every day, so price per wear, the cost of a great haircut works out well.

Second, he says, "Don't overstyle. Treat your hair almost as if you are sculpting something: look at it properly and see where, if, it is missing something. Does it need a bit of a wave here or do the ends need smoothing down? Whatever you do, don't approach it in too technical a fashion."

Third, he suggests using, "quality shampoo and conditioner. But you do not need to buy really expensive products. Obviously, I'm not saying to use shower gel on your hair, but I produced my own range because I wanted to create premium hair care at a more affordable price."

And finally, on the all-important cut, Northwood advises: "Keep it simple: you don't want too many layers but some shape around the face is always good."

Makeup

When I think of a Dior face—be it famous in one of the brand's campaigns or those of the models who stalk its catwalk—I think of freshness; of doe eyes and flushed cheeks and a pinky-nude lip. "Pretty" is not necessarily the right word because it sounds too subjective. Rather, the Dior look is dewy—it has a natural, lit-from-within glow.

Yes, you can get it at home. And it is an ideal look for daytime and evening that works on everyone, says the British makeup artist Julia Wren. Wren works with celebrities and with models on fashion campaigns and offers one-to-one tutorials with real women, so she knows her stuff. This is her guide to getting Dior skin.

SKIN PREP

Smooth the skin and tighten pores
using a gentle liquid exfoliator
followed by a rich moisturizer
for a radiant glow.

FOUNDATION

Use a dewy liquid foundation,
blending with a fluffy brush or damp
beauty sponge to keep it looking
light, sheer, and natural.

LIQUID HIGHLIGHTER

Add to the top of the cheekbones to
give an extra-natural-looking glow.

CREAMY BLUSH

Using a creamy blush in a natural pink
tone will keep the base looking fresh.

POWDER

Only on the T-zone.

BROWS

Give brows a comb and use a brow powder to gently define.

EYES

Try a wash of crème shadow or chunky eyeshadow pencil in a soft, warm brown blended over the entire lid, followed by a tight eyeliner in brown, kept to the base of the lashes and gently smudged. Next, apply a lengthening mascara for fluttery lashes.

LIPS

Achieve a soft, full pout by using a lip scrub, followed by a pretty pink balmy lipstick. For lips that need a little extra help to look full, use a liner the same shade as your own lips all over and take it just outside of the lip line. Follow with the balm.

Perfume

Dior had one rule for perfume: use it! He thought bottled scent was an essential: that each one could tell you something about its wearer. He believed it was requisite to anyone being mildly enticing (steady on, Christian) and that you shouldn't just spray it on the body—but in your entire home.

It goes without saying that we don't need to wear perfume to be attractive. Anyone who has hugged someone else, just as they are, and found it to smell like home will attest to that. But it is absolutely a wonderful thing, finding *your* fragrance. Scents evoke memories; when we think of loved ones, we can often conjure how they smell. To that end, I think Dior was right in believing that each of us should find and use a signature scent. It's not for other people, though—it is for you.

Doing so involves nothing more than trial and error. Spritz a sample of whichever perfume you want to try on your wrist and see how it wears throughout the day. If, after a few hours, you find it's a smell you want to fill your life (and wardrobe) with, you know it's yours. Apply it as lightly or liberally as you desire. But maybe don't waste it, à la Dior, scenting the spare room.

There you have it—a toolkit for a Dior-inspired life. But, before you go, I'd like to leave you with a key Dior-loved concept which we haven't yet discussed: zest.

No, not from a lemon. Zest comes from within. It's there when you exhibit a passion for something and there when you add your own finishing touches and style twists as you get dressed. It's about being both interested and interesting, but—more than that—it's about being yourself.

Nothing was more charming to Dior. He made clothes for women's bodies but was just as entranced by their minds. Remember that as you take these style principles forward. You are getting the Dior look—but you must still be *you*.

References

Oriole Cullen, *Christian Dior: Designer of Dreams*, V&A Publishing, 2019.

Christian Dior, *The Little Dictionary of Fashion*, V&A Publishing, 2008.

Christian Dior, *Dior by Dior*, V&A Publishing, 2008.

Alexander Fury, *Dior Catwalk*, Thames & Hudson, 2017.

Maria Grazia Chiuri, *Her Dior: Maria Grazia Chiuri's New Voice*, Rizzoli, 2021.

Karen Homer, *The Little Book of Dior*, Welbeck, 2020.

Florence Müller, *Grace of Monaco: Princess in Dior*, Rizzoli, 2019.

Justine Picardie, *Miss Dior: A Story of Wartime Courage and Couture*, Faber & Faber, 2021.

Elizabeth Semmelhack, *Dior by Roger Vivier*, Rizzoli, 2018.

Quote sources

p.16 Dior, Christian, quoted in: Marie, France Pochna, *Christian Dior: The Man who Made the World Look New*, Arcade Publishing, 1996, p.170.

p.36 Dior, Christian. *Gracious Quotes*. Available from: https://graciousquotes .com/christian-dior/.

p.52 Dior, Christian. *Quote Fancy*. Available from: https://quotefancy .com/quote/1164843/.

p.70 Dior, Christian. *Quote Fancy*. Available from: https://quotefancy .com/quote/1164823/.

p.88 Dior, Christian. *Goodreads*. Available from: https://www .goodreads.com/author/quotes/621328.

p.104 Dior, Christian. *AZ Quotes*. Available from: https://www.azquotes .com/quote/1074298.

p.120 Dior, Christian. *AZ Quotes*. Available from: https://www.azquotes .com/quote/542409.

p.136 Dior, Christian. *The Little Dictionary of Fashion*, V&A Publishing 2008.

p.154 Dior, Christian. *Brainy Quote*. Available from: https://www .brainyquote.com/quotes/christian _dior_636667.

p.168 Dior, Christian. *Goodreads*. Available from: https://www .goodreads.com/author/quotes/621328.

Acknowledgments

Huge thanks first to the team at Ebury, and to Ru and Lucinda in particular for your enthusiasm on this project.

To my peerless *Times* colleagues: Nicola, Anna, Harriet, Sidonie, and Hannah. Your mentoring, support, kindness, and general brilliance inspires me every day.

To the experts who made the time to bring their know-how to this book despite all possessing what I know to be immensely busy schedules! Prue, Anna, Annabel, Julia, Susan, Juanita, and George, a thousand thank yous. You have each taught me so much.

Thanks to my dear mum and dad, to my in-laws David and Lucy, to my Tormead girls, and to the JOY WhatsApp group. I could not have done this without your cheerleading.

And finally, to George, without whom I simply could not do anything.

About the Author

Hannah Rogers is *The Times*'s assistant fashion editor and stylist and covers whatever is contributing to the zeitgeist, specializing in trends, fashion, red carpet, and celebrity. She studied anthropology and sociology at Durham University, followed by an MA in fashion journalism at Central Saint Martins, and has worked in broadsheet journalism for seven years as a writer and stylist.

Picture Credits

Images kindly supplied by: Getty (p.8 CBS Photo Archive; p.12 and p.14 Bettmann; p.21 Helen H. Richardson; p.22 Michael Ochs Archives; p.25 Walter Carone (top left and right and bottom left), Bettmann (bottom right); p.27 Jeremy Moeller; p.30 Jeremy Moeller (left), Stephane Cardinale-Corbis (middle and right); p.32 Christian Vierig; p.34 Edward Berthelot; p.39 Keystone-France; p.40 Reg Lancaster; p.42 Pascal Le Segretain; p.45 Edward Berthelot; p.47 Images Press; p.48 Edward Berthelot; p.50 Pascal Le Segretain; p.55 Chevalier; p.59 Edward Berthelot; p.61 Victor Boyko; p.63 Stephane Cardinale-Corbis (left), Jeremy Moeller (right); p.64 Edward Berthelot (left and right); p.65 Stephane Cardinale-Corbis; p.66 Edward Berthelot; p.68 Edward Berthelot; p.73 Hulton Archive; p.74 Bettmann; p.79 Samir Hussein; p.80 Stephane Cardinale-Corbis; p.83 Edward Berthelot (left), Stephane Cardinale-Corbis (right); p.84 Streetstyleshooters; p.86 Gregg DeGuire; p.91 Bettmann; p.93 Keystone; p.97 Ian Gavan; p.98 Stephane Cardinale-Corbis (left), Victor Virgile (right); p.99 Jeremy Moeller (left) Victor Boyko (right); p.100 Edward Berthelot; p.102 Thierry Chesnot; p.109 Stephane De Sakutin; p.113 Stephane Cardinale-Corbis (left), Myunggu Han (right); p.114 Bryan Bedder; p.115 Marc Piasecki; p.116 Victor Virgile; p.188 Edward Berthelot; p.123 Clive Limpkin; p.125 Edward Berthelot; p.128 Victor Virgile; p.131 Edward Berthelot (left and right), Christian Vierig (middle); p.132 Edward Berthelot; p.134 Jeremy Moeller; p.141 Tim Graham; p.142 Claudio Lavenia; p.145 Streetstyleshooters; p.146 Edward Berthelot; p.150 Hanna Lassen; p.152 Streetstyleshooters; p.159 Jeremy Moeller; p.160 Amy Sussman; pp.163 and 164 Jeremy Moeller; p.166 Stephane Cardinale-Corbis; p.170 Housewife; p.174 Pascal Le Segretain; p.178 Jeremy Moeller; p.181 Stephane Cardinale-Corbis; p.182-83 Pascal Le Segretain; p.187 Claudio Lavenia); Shutterstock (endpapers Lisla); Unsplash (p.148 Osarugue Igbinoba; p.156 Camila Quintero Franco; p.157 Laura Lucas; p.173 Annie Le; p.184 Alsu Vershinina).

SIMON
ELEMENT

An Imprint of Simon & Schuster, LLC
1230 Avenue of the Americas
New York, NY 10020

First Simon Element hardcover edition March 2025

SIMON ELEMENT is a trademark of Simon & Schuster, LLC

For information about special discounts for bulk purchases, please contact Simon
& Schuster Special Sales at 1-866-506-1949 or business@simonandschuster.com.

The Simon & Schuster Speakers Bureau can bring authors to your live event. For
more information or to book an event, contact the Simon & Schuster Speakers
Bureau at 1-866-248-3049 or visit our website at www.simonspeakers.com.

Interior design by maru studio G.K.

Manufactured in Malaysia

1   3   5   7   9   10   8   6   4   2

Library of Congress Cataloging-in-Publication Data has been applied for.

ISBN 978-1-6680-8179-2
ISBN 978-1-6680-8180-8 (ebook)

This book is made from Forest Stewardship
Council® certified paper.